# Keskidee

## Integrated Language Arts for the Caribbean

# Reader 5

## Leonie Bennett

## Advisory team

| | | |
|---|---|---|
| Carol Antoine | Emma Derrick | Yvonne Forde |
| Leonise François | Sylvia Jack | Marilyn O'Brien |

## PEARSON
## Longman

### Publishing for the Caribbean

Pearson Education Limited
Edinburgh Gate, Harlow, Essex, CM20 2JE,
England and Associated Companies throughout
the world

Carlong Publishers (Caribbean) Ltd.,
P.O. Box 489, 33 Second Street, Newport West,
Kingston 13, Jamaica

First published 2004
Fifth impression 2009

Designed and typeset by Gemini Design

Illustrated by B L Kearley Ltd, London

Printed in Malaysia, VVP

## Acknowledgements

The publishers are grateful to all the copyright
owners whose material appears in this book.

## Photo Acknowledgements

We are grateful to the following for permission
to reproduce copyright photographs:

Jak Kilby/ArenaPAL for page 36; Camera Press
for page 59 top; Corbis for pages 33, 35, 51 (all),
52 (all), 53; Mary Evans Picture Library for page
14; Popperfoto.com for page 34; Redferns Music
Picture Library for page 60; Topham Picturepoint
for pages 13, 58, 59 bottom.

## Advisory Panel

The Publishers would like to thank the
following teachers and teacher trainers
for their invaluable guidance and ideas at
a series of workshops, out of which grew
Keskidee Integrated Language Arts for
the Caribbean.
Daynand Bhagirath
Arlene Black
Raffiena Boodoosingh
Pamela Boxhill
Kitts Cadette
Allison Douglas
Rosamond Estrada
Priscilla George
Yvonne Isaac
Grace King
Cindy Ramkallawa
Rae Samuel
Joseph Sanchez
Brenda Shah
Joyce Spencer
Colleen Thornton

# Contents

# Jason and the Argonauts (Part I)

## The challenge

*Jason's father had been king of Thebes. Jason's uncle Pelias had stolen the throne from his father. When Jason grew to be an adult, he came to Thebes to claim the throne back from his uncle.*

"I am the true king," Jason told Pelias.

"But how do I know you are brave and strong enough to be king of Thebes?" asked Pelias.

"I am the bravest and the strongest in the land and I will prove it to you," declared Jason. "Set me a challenge."

This was just what Pelias wanted, and he said, cunningly, "If you can bring me the famous Golden Fleece, I will give you the crown."

"I will do it!" cried Jason.

Pelias smiled to himself. He knew that the Golden Fleece was guarded by the most enormous snake which never slept. Pelias was sure Jason could not succeed in capturing the fleece.

# The adventures begin

Jason ordered a magnificent ship to be built and he called it the Argo. Then he asked all the mightiest heroes to go with him and he called them the Argonauts after his ship.

They set sail for the island of King Phineas – the only man who knew where to find the Golden Fleece. But they found that King Phineas had his own problems. Every day, at dinner time, a flock of harpies – hideous birds with women's heads – swooped over his table, snatching food and making it so filthy that there was nothing fit for the king to eat. The king was growing thinner every day.

As dinner time approached, King Phineas said to Jason, "Quick! We must hide, or the harpies will tear us apart."

"I will not hide from any man or beast," cried Jason. "I will rid you of this terrible curse."

So, when the harpies flew into the palace, the Argonauts were waiting for them. They slashed the air with their swords until it was dark with feathers and thick with the sound of squawking. Soon, the harpies were dead and the king was free.

# The clashing rocks

"Now tell us how to find the Golden Fleece," Jason demanded.

The King saw that Jason was determined and he told him that he would find the Golden Fleece on an island called Colchis.

"But, be warned," he said darkly, "no man yet has survived the clashing rocks and that is only the first of the dangers."

Next day, Jason set sail for the clashing rocks. There were two great rocks, on either side of a narrow channel, which crashed together, crushing anything that passed between them. They slowly opened and without warning hurtled towards each other once more.

"We cannot get through there!" protested the Argonauts.

But Jason had a plan. He caught a sea bird and flung it towards the rocks. Immediately the rocks smashed together.

"Now!" yelled Jason; and the Argo sped between the rocks before they had time to open and crash together again.

## Comprehension Questions

1 Why did Jason think he should be king?

2 Pelias wants Jason to:

   **a** have his crown

   **b** fail the challenge

   **c** succeed in getting the Golden Fleece

3 What form of these adjectives appears in the text: thin, brave, strong, mighty? Write out the comparative and superlative for each of these words.

4 Are the clashing rocks the only danger that Jason must face on his way to Colchis? How do you know?

5 Suggest a synonym for each of these words: sped, swooped, snatching.

**Main teaching points**
• Features of a myth   • Comparatives and superlatives

# Jason and the Argonauts (Part 2)

## Another challenge

When the Argo arrived in Colchis, Jason went to see the king of that island.

"I have come for the Golden Fleece," Jason told him. "I must have it if I am to take my place as king of Thebes."

"Of course you must have it!" laughed the king. "But first you must take on a simple challenge."

"With pleasure," said Jason, not noticing the wicked gleam in the king's eye.

"All you need do," said the king, "is to harness my two bulls, plough a field, sow the seed and gather the harvest in a single day. Then I will hand over the Golden Fleece."

"I will do it and gladly," declared Jason.

Two guards took Jason to a field in which there stood two powerful bulls. As Jason approached, the bulls began to snort. Steam and flames poured from their nostrils; the guards laughed and left. Jason leaped backwards in fright, and found himself in the arms of Medea, the king's daughter.

Medea had been watching Jason since he arrived on the island and had quickly fallen in love with the brave and handsome youth.

"I have magic powers," she whispered, "and I will help you whenever you need me." With that, she gave him a cloak which protected him from the bull's fiery breath. Jason threw the cloak about his shoulders and, thus protected, he harnessed the creatures and ploughed the field. Then he began to sow the seed that the guards had given him.

Jason did not know it, but the king had mixed dragon's teeth with the seeds and, as each tooth hit the soil, it sprouted into a fierce warrior. Soon there were hundreds of warriors in the field, their swords glinting, all eager for Jason's blood.

"We must fight for our lives!" cried Jason to the Argonauts – and they did not let him down. They roared and slashed and stabbed for hour after hour until, at the end of the day, every one of the dragon-tooth warriors lay dead.

# The Golden Fleece

Now the king had no choice and he led Jason to the garden of the Golden Fleece. "There it is," he scoffed. "But no man will ever get past the snake which guards it."

Jason stared at the terrifying creature. Its fangs were deadly needles, full of poison; its scales were as sharp as daggers. It was longer than the longest river and broader than the mightiest tree.

The king chuckled and left Jason to his fate.

"Fear not," whispered Medea in his ear. "I can help you."

From her robe she produced a powerful sleeping potion which she handed to Jason. Summoning up all his courage, he approached this deadliest of monsters.

The snake drew itself up to the height of a mountain. Its great mouth opened like a great cave, then its huge, hissing head darted down towards Jason. Quick as lightning, he threw the potion into the monstrous mouth.

Within seconds, the snake tumbled to the ground asleep and the earth trembled with the shock of its fall.

Jason raced back down to the sea shore and leaped aboard the Argo. By his side, was Medea, his future bride. Over his arm was the softest, most brilliant fleece in all the world.

"Set sail for Thebes!" he called to the Argonauts. "Now, I will be king!"

And so he was.

## Comprehension Questions

1 What form of these adjectives appears in the text: long, broad, deadly, soft, brilliant? Write out the comparative and superlative of each one.

2 What do you understand by these phrases: 'thus protected', 'his future bride'?

3 Find a word or phrase which means the same as each of these words: sorceress, youth, chuckled, potion.

4 The dragons'-tooth warriors wanted to:

   a  kill the bulls

   b  drink Jason's blood

   c  kill Jason

5 Summarise the complete story by using one or two sentences to say what happens in each of the 5 sections.

6 "Summoning up all his courage, he approached this deadliest of monsters." How would you say this if you were writing a modern-day story?

**Main teaching points**
• Comparatives and superlatives   • Summary

# Flood!

It was already raining when I woke up that morning, and I remember looking out of the window before I went to school. All the flowers that Mummy had planted in pots and cans had been battered by the rain, and the yard was spattered with red and orange petals.

   I ran to school with my bag over my head wondering why people tried to go anywhere in their cars when it was raining. They wanted to keep dry, but there were so many of them that they were all stuck in one enormous traffic jam. The drivers were hooting their horns and shouting at each other, and I laughed as I overtook them. The drains in the street were overflowing and I was jumping in and out and through and over the most enormous puddles.

It continued to rain all day, and on the way home I had to wade through water over my ankles. My shoes were new and I didn't want them to get ruined so I took them off and carried them. There were not so many cars out now but quite a few had been abandoned. Branches and newspapers and other rubbish had been washed up against gates and fences, and I enjoyed the feeling of everything being strange and different.

Then I turned the corner into my street and gulped – it looked like the sea. Water was lapping round the houses. There were real waves and someone paddled past me in a boat! A plastic chair floated by and I began to get worried. What if all our furniture was washed away along with the computer and the TV and my collection of space monsters? The water was up to my knees now. I tried to run home, but you can't run in very deep water so I just had to wade as fast as I could. All the time I was thinking of bad things that might have happened. Maybe I would get back and there would be nobody in the house and I wouldn't know where to go to find Mummy and Daddy and my little sister Tamara. My chest felt tight and my head was hurting, and then, suddenly, I heard someone shout my name.

There was Daddy, wading towards me with Tamara on his shoulders. She was hanging onto his ears and laughing so hard her red plastic rain hat had slipped over her eyes.

Daddy gave me a hug and told me that Mummy and the house were fine. There were three steps up to our front door and they were enough to make sure that the water didn't get in. But, just in case, he and Mummy had moved the TV and the computer and my collection of space monsters upstairs to the bedroom.

By bedtime the rain had stopped and, next morning, the sun came out and the clearing up began.

## Comprehension Questions

1 Why did the writer laugh on his way to school?

2 Write what you think Daddy said to the writer when they met. Use speech marks.

3 What do you think the writer felt when 'someone paddled past [him] in a boat'?

4 The writer's head was hurting because:

a he was frightened

b he had a headache

c he had bumped it

5 Why was everything in the writer's house fine?

6 How do the writer's feelings change through the day?

**Main teaching points**
• Passive voice

9

# Walking home alone

When you're walking home alone
Shadows dart
 and jump and bump
 up against you so you back into the bush

There are branches that will
Stab you and grab you

When it's dark, remark
How the noises bite
 and tease and squeeze
 and make you feel that there's something out there that is

Fierce that will pierce
With a knife your life
Or will scare you half to death.          **Leonie Bennett**

# Moon-Gazer

On moonlight night
When moon is bright
Beware, Beware –

Moon-Gazer man
With his throw-back head
And his open legs
Gazing, gazing
Up at the moon

Moon-Gazer man
With his seal-skin hair
And his round-eye stare
Staring, staring
Up at the moon

Moon-Gazer man
Standing tall,
Lamp-post tall,
Just gazing up
At moon eye-ball

But never try to pass
Between those open legs
Cause Moon-Gazer man
Will close them with a snap – you'll be trapped

Moon-Gazer man
Will crush you flat.
Yes, with just one shake
Suddenly you'll be a human pancake

On moonlight night
When moon is bright
For goodness' sake
Stay home –
And pull your window-curtain tight.

**Grace Nichols**

*Moon-Gazer is a supernatural folk-figure, extremely tall, who could be seen mostly straddling roadways on moonlit nights, gazing up at the moon. It is best to avoid passing between his legs.*

## Comprehension Questions

**Walking home alone**

1  Do noises really bite? Do shadows really bump against you? Why do you think the poet says they do?

2  What does 'remark' mean in the poem?

3  Does the poem remind you of anything or any way you have ever felt? Describe the feelings you had.

**Moon-Gazer**

4  What must you never do? Why?

5  Make each of these phrases into a simile:

   **a**  seal-skin hair

   **b**  lamp-post tall

   **c**  moon eye-ball

6  Why do you think the poet repeats the words 'beware', 'gazing' and 'staring'?

7  Reread the last verse. How does the last line make you feel?

8  Read both poems aloud. Make them sound scary.

**Main teaching points**
• Reading aloud   • Use of language

# Blackbeard the pirate

When piracy was at its height, Blackbeard was the most famous and most feared pirate of all.

Blackbeard's real name was Edward Teach and people think he was an Englishman. His career as a pirate began around 1713, when he became a crewman on a Jamaican pirate ship. He was soon made commander of his own ship. In November 1717 he captured a ship which was taking slaves from West Africa to St. Vincent. He called this ship the *Queen Anne's Revenge* and she became his flagship. She was one of the largest pirate ships ever, carrying 150 pirates and 40 big guns.

The sight of Blackbeard was enough to make most of his victims surrender without a fight. If they gave up peacefully, he would usually take their valuables and their rum and then allow them to sail away. If they tried to fight, he would often maroon their crews on an island and burn their ship. Although he was seen as dangerous and devilish, as far as we know, Blackbeard never killed anyone who was not trying to kill him.

During the winter of 1717–1718 the *Queen Anne's Revenge* sailed round the Caribbean taking 'prizes' on the way. It is said that Blackbeard took 18 ships in seven months and kept three of them. By the time he was sailing north up the American coast in spring 1718, he was in command of four ships and over 300 pirates.

After the *Queen Anne's Revenge* ran aground in North Carolina, Blackbeard escaped with a small group of men and the valuables that they had recently taken. But he was not free for long.

The British Navy caught up with Blackbeard and killed him in a brief but bloody battle on 22nd November 1718. He is said to have been so strong that it took five musketball wounds and more than 20 sword wounds to kill him.

**Blackbeard's own words:**

Here is a note, said to be written by Blackbeard. It was found on one of his ships after his death:

*Such a day, rum all out: –*
*Our company somewhat sober: –*
*A damned confusion amongst us!*
*Rogues a plotting: – Great talk of*
*separation – so I looked sharp for*
*a prize: – Such a day found one*
*with a great deal of liquor on*
*board, so kept the company hot,*
*damned hot; then all things went*
*well again.*

# The wreck of Blackbeard's ship

In 1996, the wreck of Blackbeard's flagship, the *Queen Anne's Revenge*, was discovered off the coast of North Carolina. She was lying beneath 20 feet of water and buried under sand with only an anchor showing. Many things have been found, including the barrel of a blunderbuss and some 24-pounder cannonballs.

## Comprehension Questions

1 Find these words in the text: crewman, flagship, valuables, prizes, stamp out. What do you think they mean? Make up your own definitions for them. Then check them in the dictionary or with your teacher.

2 Reread 'Blackbeard's own words'. What does he mean by these words and phrases:
  a 'rum all out'          b 'sober'
  c 'rogues a-plotting'    d 'a prize'
  e 'liquor'               f 'kept the company hot'

3 Write your own version of Blackbeard's note, making it easier to understand.

4 Did Blackbeard ever kill anyone and, if so, whom did he kill?

5 Blackbeard was killed in a 'brief but bloody battle'. What sort of battle was this?

6 What do you think the life of a pirate was like? Imagine you were a 'crewman' and describe your life.

**Main teaching points**
• Nouns  • Unfamiliar vocabulary

# Why we see what we see

## Optical illusions

What we see is affected by our eyes and our brains. Sometimes our brains are confused by an image. When that happens we may think we see one thing – but, a moment later, we see something completely different!

When this happens, we talk about an 'optical illusion'. Look at picture 1. Do you see a vase or two faces? They are both there, but they cannot be seen at the same time.

Now look at picture 2. Some people see a duck while some people see a rabbit. What you see depends on what part of the picture you focus on. When your brain has become used to it you can focus on one image and then on another. Try it.

Sometimes our brains are fooled by what is around the image.

In picture 3, the red circle on the left looks bigger than the red circle on the right. When it is measured, we discover that the two circles are the same size.

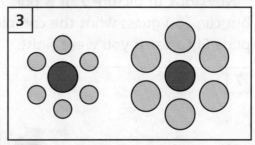

Look at picture 4. Which vertical line is longer? Now measure them. Why do you think the one on the left looks longer?

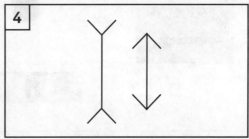

**optical illusions**
- Find out the meaning of 'optical'.
- Find out the meaning of 'illusion'.
- Explain to a partner what an optical illusion is.

## The eyes and brain work together

We use what we know to help us understand what we see. You don't need a lot of information to understand a picture. Your brain will try to make sense of what little information it has. Any gaps will be filled by using your memory.

Look at picture 5. It is like a jigsaw with some of the pieces missing. Your eyes and brain will work together to help you work out that it is a heart.

Look at the shapes below. What do you think they are? Why do you think that? See page 61 to find out if you were right.

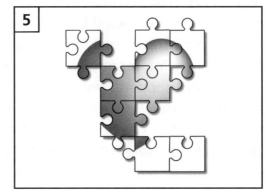

Now look at picture 7. It is part of a photograph. A lot of it is missing, but can you guess what the complete picture would look like? Look at page 61 to see if you were right.

# How movies work

Did you know that movies are made up of thousands and thousands of still pictures? They only seem to be moving. Each picture is just a tiny bit different from the one before and the one after it. When we watch a movie, all these pictures are projected onto a screen one after the other very quickly so that each picture is seen for just a fraction of a second. Our brains try to make sense of them and tell us that they are moving.

A simple way of testing this out is with a flick book. The diagram below tells you how to make one.

Looking at optical illusions is fun but it also has a serious side. Scientists study them carefully to find out how the brain and the eyes work together.

## Comprehension Questions

1 'We use what we know to help us understand what we see.' Explain to a partner what you understand this sentence to mean.

2 Give a friend clear instructions on how to make a flick book. Use the diagrams to help you.

3 List all the verbs in this text which are in the passive voice.

4 Rewrite all the sentences you found that contain the passive voice. Make them active.

5 What does 'little information' mean?

  a information about small things

  b not much information

  c small signposts

# The new boy

Sanjay had arrived early for school. There were no other kids around so he hung out in the yard kicking stones at an empty cola can.

"Goal!" he yelled, when at last he hit it.

"Good shot!" said a voice he didn't recognise.

He spun round to face the speaker – a boy whose face was so perfect it looked like a mask. The boy held out his hand.

"My name's Jonas," he said. "I'm new."

There was something odd about his voice. It was smooth like syrup. Sanjay had heard voices like that on television advertisements. Reluctantly, he shook hands with the boy, thinking, '*Nobody* shakes hands – *ever!*'
"Which class are you going into?" he asked.

"Miss King's Class," Jonas replied.

"Same as me," said Sanjay. He smiled at Jonas, remembering what it was like to be a new boy. "Can you hit that can?"

"Of course," said Jonas, lining up a stone with his foot.

"Wow!" gasped Sanjay.

The stone had left Jonas' foot like a bullet. It had passed straight through the can and out the other side before hitting the wall.

Sanjay stared at the new boy in amazement, and only then did he notice Jonas' clothes. He was wearing the school colours, but it looked as if they had been painted onto him. Sanjay wanted to reach out and touch the smooth, shiny surface of Jonas' arm. He was sure it would feel like plastic.

Now, Sanjay was beginning to feel uneasy. "What school were you at before?" he asked.

"It was a very long way away," Jonas replied, mysteriously.

"On another island?" asked Sanjay.

"On another planet," said Jonas, without smiling.

'Strange sense of humour,' thought Sanjay, laughing nervously.

"Watch out!" shouted Jonas, suddenly.

"What is it?" asked Sanjay, looking around.

Jonas pointed to Sanjay's school bag. "Your chocolate drink is leaking and making a mess of your books."

Sanjay grabbed his bag and pulled it open. Jonas was right. There was chocolate milk all over his reading book and his notebook. Miss King would go mad.

Then he stared at Jonas. "How did you know?" he demanded. "You can't see into my bag ... can you?"

Jonas didn't answer.

Sanjay tipped his books out and started wiping them on his shirt front.

"What's up?" called a voice he knew. He looked up and there was his friend, Marissa.

"Marissa, meet Jonas," he said.

But Jonas was nowhere to be seen. "He's a new boy and he was here a moment ago."

"Well, he isn't here now," said Marissa.

"He's in our class so you'll see him later."

But Jonas wasn't in class and, when Sanjay asked Miss King about him she said, "No, there's no new boy starting today – not in this class or in any other class."

"But I saw him."

"You must have imagined it," said Miss King, smiling.

At break, Sanjay went out into the yard and found the old cola can. There was a hole right through it. So he hadn't imagined it.

But who was Jonas? Where did he come from ... and would he ever come back?

## Comprehension Questions

1  Find 4 similes.

2  Find 4 past participles.

3  List 3 things that are strange about Jonas.

4  Who do you think Jonas is? Where do you think he may have come from?

5  Why do you think the writer tells us that Sanjay was 'remembering what it was like to be a new boy'?

6  Imagine that Jonas comes back. What happens? Tell the story to a friend.

**Main teaching points**
• Past plus past participle  • Similes

# Compere Lapin pays a price
## (Part I)

by Jacintha A Lee

Compere Lapin could not stand gossip. He always got really annoyed any time he came across a group of animals discussing other people's affairs.

"But what wrong with them? They only talking about other people," said his friends.

Compere Lapin tried telling them that this was a bad habit to indulge in, but they only teased him.

Compere Lapin started getting really angry. He decided to ask God a favour.

"Mr. God, these animals really talk a lot you know – teach them a lesson. Any time they talk about anyone let them fall unconscious for one hour."

God granted him that favour. Next day, Compere Lapin filled a basket with all kinds of plants and seeds. There were yams, lettuce, cabbage, potatoes, dasheen and many others. These he started planting on a piece of hard, dry rock, singing away as he worked.

A few minutes later, Compere Tigre passed by. He could not believe his eyes. What was Compere Lapin doing on this dry place!

"Compere Lapin," he called out. "Man what you doing there?"

"Well, compere, I just planting a bit of food. You know how things hard these days," Lapin sang out, but still working away.

Compere Tigre scratched his chin and moved away.

"You mean to tell me on this rock Lapin go plant food? The man must be going ma … a … aa … a …"

Compere Lapin smiled as Compere Tigre fell unconscious to the ground.

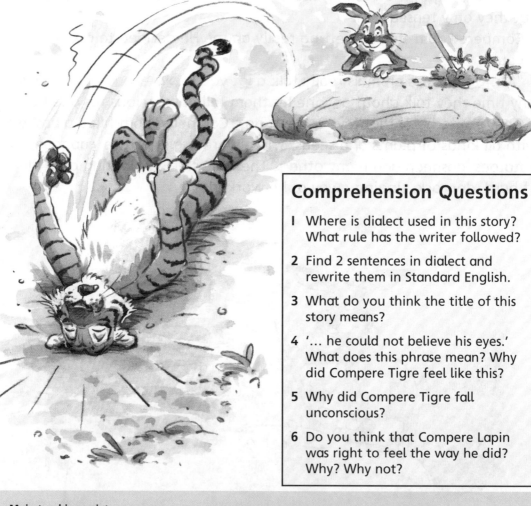

## Comprehension Questions

1 Where is dialect used in this story? What rule has the writer followed?

2 Find 2 sentences in dialect and rewrite them in Standard English.

3 What do you think the title of this story means?

4 '… he could not believe his eyes.' What does this phrase mean? Why did Compere Tigre feel like this?

5 Why did Compere Tigre fall unconscious?

6 Do you think that Compere Lapin was right to feel the way he did? Why? Why not?

**Main teaching points**
• Appropriate use of dialect

23

# Compere Lapin pays a price
## (Part 2)

by Jacintha A Lee

*Compere Tigre fell unconscious and Compere Lapin smiled …*

"Aha!" he breathed out. "That is one that go mind he business later on."
He then placed Compere Tigre under the naked sun.

"One whole hour of this go make him regret he said that about me."

Compere Lapin sat under the shade of a tree and waited until the hour was up. Tigre got up frowning. He could not understand what he was doing there. His eyes were sore, his lips were dry, some of the hair on his body had even got burned. Tigre rubbed his eyes and looked at Lapin.

"Compere, what happen to me?"

"Well, Compere, that was a lesson on minding you business."

"Bu … bu … bu … bu," Compere Tigre stammered.

"If you tell the others why you in this state, the same thing go happen to you again," Compere warned him.

"Okay Compere, I eh go tell nobody," Compere Tigre, said as he limped away.

Compere Lapin smiled and looked around to see whether there was a new victim in sight. He saw no one, not even Compere Pigeon who sat on the tree above him. Pigeon had seen everything that had taken place!

Every day a different animal suffered the same fate as Compere Tigre. They could not warn the others for fear of a repeat. After a few days, Compere Pigeon decided to make his appearance. He placed a towel over his back and passed near Lapin. He said nothing except, "Good morning Compere," and continued on his way.

Compere Lapin stopped and frowned. "That funny," he said to himself. "Compere Pigeon," he called out, "I there working hard. I planting something here so that I go get some food later on."

"Work away, Compere. I myself going for a bath and a trim. See you Compere." Pigeon walked daintily away. Compere Lapin could not believe his eyes and ears, he shook his head slowly.

"Ah! Ah! Pigeon really fresh you know. You mean to tell me Pigeon have hair on that bald head of his for him to trim? He head looking like a … a … a … a … a …"

Compere Lapin could not understand why the trees were dancing around him, why the ground was getting closer, closer, closer and closer.

Compere Pigeon, a little distance off, smiled as he saw Compere Lapin fall to the ground. He ran to the spot and said to the unconscious Lapin, "Do unto others as you want them to do to you, Compere."

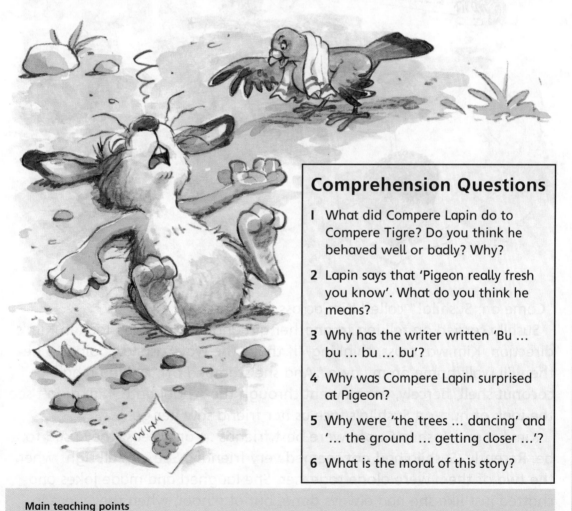

## Comprehension Questions

1 What did Compere Lapin do to Compere Tigre? Do you think he behaved well or badly? Why?

2 Lapin says that 'Pigeon really fresh you know'. What do you think he means?

3 Why has the writer written 'Bu … bu … bu … bu'?

4 Why was Compere Lapin surprised at Pigeon?

5 Why were 'the trees … dancing' and '… the ground … getting closer …'?

6 What is the moral of this story?

**Main teaching points**
• Speech marks

# Friends

"Come on, Sushila!" called Kim across the classroom.

Sushila carried on talking to another girl and did not even look in Kim's direction. Kim was cross, thinking, 'if that's the way Sushila's going to be then I'll walk home on my own.' And she stomped off, kicking a half coconut shell, fiercely, as she went through the school gate. Kim didn't see the look of hurt on Sushila's face as her friend saw her go.

Kim Lai and Sushila Gupta were best friends … or at least they used to be. Recently, Sushila had not seemed very friendly. She was all right when the two of them were alone together. She laughed and made jokes and chatted just like she had always done, but at school, when they were in the classroom or in the playground, Sushila often ignored Kim.

"I don't think Sushila likes me any more," Kim told her mum, when they were peeling yams in the kitchen.

"She doesn't even laugh when I whisper silly things in class," she told her dad when they were down at the market.

Mum and Dad were sympathetic. "Perhaps she's got a new friend," suggested Mum, wiping her hands on her apron and picking up a knife to start chopping.

"Have you had a row?" asked Dad, as he paid the man at the fish stall for three red snappers.

"No! Nothing like that's happened!" said Kim to both of them.

Dad was sorry to see Kim so upset, and later he asked Mum, "Why don't you have a word with Mrs. Gupta?"

"Good idea," said Mum. "Maybe she knows what's wrong."

A few days later, the two mums met and Mrs. Gupta told Kim's mum that she was worried about Sushila. She said that Sushila seemed to have changed. "She has always been such a good girl, but now she doesn't listen to what I say. When I call her she doesn't come and sometimes she ignores me completely – it's like living with the worst teenager, but she's only 10 years old!"

"Oh dear," said Mrs. Lai, sympathetically. "That does sound difficult."

"And she's not very happy," Mrs Gupta went on. "She says that Kim isn't as friendly as she used to be and often goes off without her."

Kim's mum and Sushila's mum chatted for a bit longer and agreed that they would talk again soon. That evening, over supper, Mum told Kim and her dad about her talk with Mrs. Gupta. Dad looked thoughtful.

After a few minutes he said, hesitantly, "I used to teach a boy who behaved a bit like Sushila. He was fine when you were standing close to him, but he appeared to ignore people when they were further away or if there was a noise going on."

"What was wrong?" asked Kim.

"It turned out he had a hearing problem. He couldn't hear unless people were right next to him. But he saw a doctor and got lots of help and now he's doing fine again in the senior school," Dad replied.

"Do you think Sushila might have a hearing problem?" asked Kim.

"I don't know," said Dad, "but it would be worth having it checked out."

* * *

It turned out that Kim's Dad was right. Sushila went to the hospital and was diagnosed with a hearing problem.

A month later, Kim and Sushila were walking home arm in arm, when Kim turned to Sushila, saying, "Why didn't you tell me you couldn't hear properly?"

"I didn't know I was missing anything," protested Sushila. "I just knew that Mum kept shouting at me and you kept going off without me."

"Well now the doctors are going to help you," smiled Kim, giving her a hug. "And we're always going to be friends."

## Comprehension Questions

1 What does each of these words mean: sympathetic, diagnosed, protested? Use each one in a sentence of your own.

2 "Kim didn't see the look of hurt on Sushila's face as her friend saw her go." Explain what has happened and why.

3 How had Sushila changed?

4 Sushila was ignoring her friend and her mum because:

   a she was angry with them

   b she was a teenager

   c she didn't always hear when they spoke to her

5 Explain why there is a break in the text. (* * *)

6 What do you think happened next?

**Main teaching points**
• Talking about disabilities   • Talking about friendship

30

# Lost cities

We have known about the lost city of Atlantis since the time of Plato, 2000 years ago, but did you know that more 'lost' cities have been discovered recently? Here are some of the newspaper articles which announced the finds.

## Underwater city near Cuba

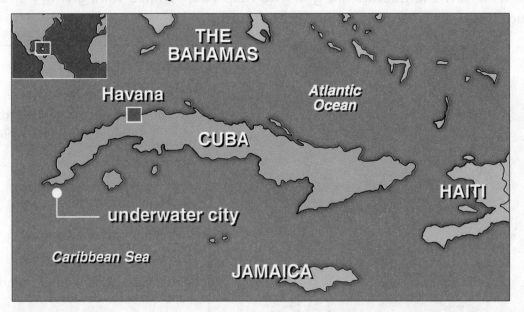

**December 2001**

A team of explorers have made an unexpected find near the west coast of Cuba. They have discovered what they think are the ruins of a submerged city, built thousands of years ago.

The explorers first spotted the underwater city last year when their scanners showed images of unusual stone structures. Some of the blocks were built in pyramid shapes, others were circular, researchers said.

"It is not impossible that these structures were built more than 6000 years ago," said one of the explorers, "which would make them 1500 years older than the pyramids. However, we need a lot more evidence before we can be sure of what we have found." ❏

# Explorer finds lost city

ECUADOR
COLOMBIA
■ Saposoa
BRAZIL
Lima ■
PERU
THE ANDES
BOLIVIA
Pacific
Ocean

## June 2000

An explorer, Gene Savoy, says he has discovered a lost city deep in the rainforest of Peru. The explorer and his team believe they have uncovered one of the lost cities of the Chachapoyas people who moved to eastern Peru about AD 700.

Some members of the team even say this might be the city of El Dorado – the city of gold – about which there are so many stories.

Savoy insists that no gold has been found, but he refuses to say where the city is in case it attracts thieves.

The team have begun to uncover a stone city, which contains up to 150 buildings, including houses, temples and burial sites. There are also stone roads and at least 36 burial towers. The explorers' next job is to carefully scrape away the thick jungle vegetation to disclose more details about this long-hidden city.

Over the last 40 years, Gene Savoy and his team of archaeologists have found several other settlements built by the Chachapoyas. One of them was made up of 20,000 stone buildings and is thought to be the capital of the Chachapoyas empire. ❏

# Divers find pharaohs' lost city

A statue of goddess Isis was found in the harbour in 1998.

**June 2000**

Underwater archaeologists have discovered a submerged city off the coast of Egypt. They think it is the ancient city of Herakleion, which was Egypt's main port in the time of the pharaohs.

People have always known that there was a city of Herakleion and they knew that the city disappeared over a thousand years ago. But no one had seen evidence of it and no one knew why it vanished under the water. Scientists are hoping that this amazing new discovery will give them answers to some of their questions.

Herakleion was rediscovered in waters six to nine metres deep. Beneath the water, divers have found a lost world untouched by time, full of temples, houses, huge statues and a store of gold coins and jewellery. Team diver Eric Smith said, "After just a couple of dives, we discovered so many objects – the site is rich and amazing." As many as 20,000 pieces are reported to be still on the sea floor.

Archaeologists are now hoping to work out from the ruins how people lived in this ancient and almost forgotten city. ❏

## Comprehension Questions

1 Find words beginning with the prefixes: dis-, un-, im-, re-, sub-.
Write your own definition of each word. Then check it in the dictionary.

2 "… we need … more evidence before we can be sure what we have found."
What sort of 'evidence' might they find? Why do they need lots of evidence?

3 In the third article, what do you think are the questions to which the scientists want answers?

4 What does the phrase 'a lost world untouched by time' mean?

5 How do you think archaeologists can 'work out from the ruins' how people lived?

6 If you found a lost city, what sort of 'evidence' would you like to find? Why?

**Main teaching points**
• Common prefixes dis- un- im- re- sub-

# It started with calypso ...

People all over the world love Afro-Caribbean music. You probably know the names of several different types, but did you know that it all began with calypso?

When the first slaves came from West Africa, they brought their folk songs, called *kaiso*, with them. Life was hard on the plantations of Trinidad and Tobago, and the slaves used to sing the songs from back home to help them to feel strong and united. They also used the songs as a way of talking about the masters they hated and to remember the places they came from. They changed the words of the songs to suit their new lives, and gradually the African folk songs developed into what became known as calypso.

## The first calypso hits

Calypso singing carried on long after slavery was abolished, but it continued to develop and change. Calypso began to borrow from American jazz and popular music and soon it was being sung outside the Caribbean. The first calypso recording was made in New York in 1912 and, after that, calypso spread far and wide. There were many famous calypsonians – in particular, Lord Kitchener who was the best-known calypso singer from the 1940s through to the 50s and 60s.

**Lord Kitchener**

In 1956, a singer called Harry Belafonte recorded an album which included the Banana Boat Song, *Day-O*. This became the first calypso album to sell over one million copies and in this same year a singer known as the Mighty Sparrow became the king of calypso with a song called *Jean and Dinah*.

In a recent interview, a calypsonian called Brother Valentino explained that, in his opinion, a calypso must always have a lesson or a message – rather like a moral in a story. This is what he said about the songs he writes:

**Harry Belafonte**

*"I always like to choose a topic you could get a message from ..."*

He went on to say that he thinks young people are not very interested in calypso any more:

*"Calypso is like story telling ... It takes a lot of thought and I don't think many young people want to think too much ... It is sad to see that calypso cannot attract young people."*

The interviewer asked Brother Valentino if a calypso singer should make people feel that they have hope and can change things in the world. Valentino answered:

*"DEFINITELY. AND THAT IS MY ROLE ... I like to be direct and positive, instead of being negative or indirect. Music should dictate what direction the nation is going ..."*

## Soca

People say that soul and calypso were combined in Trinidad to form a new style of music called soca, which quickly became very popular. Soca mixed traditional calypso music with East Indian rhythms, bringing together the music of the two largest groups in Trinidad, the Africans and East Indians. This new up-beat tempo quickly became popular.

**Arrow is a famous Soca singer from Montserrat**

## Jamaican music

From Jamaica came another stream of Afro-Caribbean music – ska, followed by rock steady and reggae – but that's another story.

## Comprehension Questions

1  Why did slaves sing songs from back home?

2  What does it mean that the Mighty Sparrow 'was the king of calypso'?

3  What do we call someone who sings calypso?

4  In 4 sentences, summarise the history of Afro Caribbean music from kaiso to soca.

5  Brother Valentino thinks young people today:

   a  like calypso

   b  like sending messages

   c  don't like thinking

6  Do you agree with Brother Valentino? Explain why or why not.

**Main teaching points**
• Summary

# Good Mother and The Enormous Elephant

## A play, based on a story from Africa

## Characters

Good Mother
Neighbour 1
Neighbour 2
Antelope
Leopard
The Enormous Elephant
Child 1
Child 2
Narrator

## Scene 1 – *in the jungle*

| | |
|---|---|
| **Neighbour 1:** | What are you doing, Good Mother? |
| **Good Mother:** | I'm building a house for me and my children. |
| **Neighbour 2:** | But you can't build it there, in the middle of the road. That's the animals' road. The leopards, the antelopes and the elephants will be furious. |
| **Good Mother:** | This is the best place for me and my children. There is space for them to play and light for them to grow up in. I am not afraid of the animals. |
| *(2 days later)* | |
| **Good Mother:** | Now children, I'm going out to collect firewood. While I am gone, you must stay indoors. Whatever you do, don't play on the animals' road. |
| **Children:** | Yes, mama. |

| | |
|---|---|
| **Narrator:** | Good Mother goes off into the bush and, straightaway, the children come out and play on the road. An antelope appears. |
| **Antelope:** | Whose children are you? |
| **Children:** | We are Good Mother's children. |
| **Antelope:** | You are beautiful children, I am happy to see you. |
| **Narrator:** | The antelope wanders off to graze in the bush and a leopard appears. |
| **Leopard:** | Whose children are you? |
| **Children:** | We are Good Mother's children. |
| **Leopard:** | You are handsome children, I am happy to see you. |
| **Narrator:** | The leopard slopes off to doze on a low branch and an enormous elephant comes crashing down the road, bellowing angrily. |
| **Elephant:** | Whose children are you? |
| **Children:** | We are Good Mother's children. |
| **Elephant:** | You are wicked children, playing in the middle of my road, so I am going to eat you up! |

**Narrator:** The elephant gathers up the children in his trunk and swallows them whole. When the neighbours come running out of their houses shouting, he gobbles them up too then he lumbers off down the road. A few minutes later Good Mother reappears.

**Good Mother:** Where are my children?

**Leopard:** The elephant was angry because they were in the middle of his road so he devoured them.

**Good Mother:** Aieeeeeeeeee! My precious children! Aieeeeeeeeee! I must rescue my sweet children. What can I do?

**Leopard:** There is nothing you can do. Your children are lost and you must forget about them. I have lost many children.

**Good Mother:** I will not give up so easily. I will go after the elephant and I will rescue my clever, happy children.

**Narrator:** Good Mother walks along the animals' road for many miles until, at last, she comes across The Enormous Elephant, drinking at a muddy pool.

**Good Mother:** Are you the wicked creature that gobbled up my beautiful children?

**Elephant:** Certainly not! I never eat children. They give me indigestion. The elephant you want is further down the road.

**Good Mother:** I don't believe you. I can see lumps and bumps moving about inside your elephant belly.

**Elephant:** You are imagining things.

**Narrator:** Good Mother moves closer to the elephant to inspect its bulging belly.

**Good Mother:** Look at that bulge.
Do you think I don't know the shape of my own beautiful child's foot?
My precious children are inside your insides.

**Elephant:** Do you wish to see them again?

**Good Mother:** Yes! Right now!

**Elephant:** In that case … in you go!

**Narrator:** The elephant whooshes Good Mother into his mouth and swallows her whole.

## Comprehension Questions

1 What sort of person is Good Mother? How do you know?

2 Why does the leopard say, "I have lost many children."?

3 In what way is the antelope's character different from that of Good Mother? Which words tell you?

4 List all the adjectives used to describe Good Mother's children.

5 What sort of character is The Enormous Elephant? How do you know?

6 What do you think will happen next? Write the narrator's next speech.

# Good Mother and The Enormous Elephant

## Scene 2 – inside The Enormous Elephant

**Good Mother:** It's very dark in here. I can't see anything. (*shouting*) Hello! HELLO! Is anybody there?

**Neighbour 1:** (*almost in tears*) Is that you, Good Mother? Has The Enormous Elephant eaten you too? What a terrible fate has befallen us!

**Neighbour 2:** (*wailing*) We will never escape. We are doomed to starve to death here inside the elephant's belly.

**Good Mother:** (*sharply*) Stop moaning and groaning. No one is doomed. I have come to find my beautiful children. Tell me where they are. Quickly!

**Neighbour 1:** I heard them crying, poor things. How dreadful for them, to lose their lives so young.

**Good Mother:** Stop whining and sorrowing. No one has lost their lives yet.

**Narrator:** Good Mother begins to walk all round the elephant's belly, sloshing through warm muddy river water, searching for her children and calling their names. Then she hears their voices.

**Child 1:** Mama! Mama! We are here!

**Child 2:** We knew you would come and find us.

**Good Mother:** (*throwing her arms around her children*) Oh what happiness!

**Neighbour 1:** How can you talk about happiness when we are trapped inside an elephant's belly?

**Neighbour 2:** Trapped without hope of escape.

**Good Mother:** As long as we are alive and have each other there is hope. I feared I would never see my beautiful children and my good neighbours again, and now here we are all together once more. We should celebrate!

**Narrator:** The woman and her children all jump up and down for joy.

**Elephant:** Woman be still! You are giving me a bellyache with all your stamping and tramping about inside my insides.

**Good Mother:** 'Be still', did you say? 'A bellyache', did you say? Just you wait, you wicked, child-eating elephant. Come on neighbours, let's jump! Come on children, let's dance for joy!

**Narrator:** So Good Mother and the neighbours and the children dance and jump and stomp about for all they are worth.

**Elephant:** Stop it! Stop jumping! My guts are grinding; my belly is bumping; my insides are in terrible pain.

**Good Mother:** Keep jumping children! Keep dancing neighbours!

| | |
|---|---|
| **Elephant:** | Aaaaaaagh! Have pity! |
| **Good Mother:** | Leap higher neighbours! Kick your feet, children! |
| **Elephant:** | Eurghhhhhhhhhhhhh! I cannot stand it any more. I think I am going to be sick … |
| **Narrator:** | The elephant cannot keep Good Mother and her children and the neighbours inside his stomach any longer. |
| **Elephant:** | Eeeeurghhhhhh! |
| **Narrator:** | Out they all shoot through his mouth on a warm river of muddy water, along with everything else the elephant has eaten this day. |
| **Elephant:** | Ooooooooooh! My poor belly. |
| **Good Mother:** | It serves you right for eating innocent children. |
| **Elephant:** | Oooooooh! My insides are so sore. I swear I will never eat women and children again. They are too much trouble. |
| **Good Mother:** | I am glad to hear you have learned at least one lesson. Now, come on, neighbours, let's go home. |
| **Narrator:** | Good Mother and her children and her neighbours went back down the road and lived ever after in peace with their friends the animals. |

## Comprehension Questions

1 Rewrite the first 2 speeches as reported speech. Begin *'Good Mother said that it was …'*

2 Practise reading the first 4 speeches, taking notice of the stage directions (the words in brackets).

3 Write out Elephant's and Good Mother's last 2 speeches, adding your own stage directions.

4 What lesson do you think the neighbours might have learned?

5 Do you feel sorry for the elephant? Why? Why not?

6 Practise reading the play aloud in groups. Use lots of expression. Then perform the play for the rest of the class.

**Main teaching points**
• Reported speech   • Features of a play

# The spelling test

## Part 1

Jake and Zanna were practising for a spelling test.

"How do you spell cough?" asked Jake.

"That's easy. It's one of those 'ough' words like rough," laughed Zanna.

"All right, then, Miss Clever," said Jake with a sneaky smile. "Spell 'necessary'."

Zanna's face twisted with concentration. "N-e-s ..." she began, then shook her head and began again. "N-e-c-c-e-s ... Is it one 's' or two?"

"Not telling," said Jake, enjoying her discomfort.

Zanna was Jake's twin sister and she always did better than him in tests. It was not that she was cleverer than him; it was just that she was better at taking tests. He always got so nervous he could not think straight and everything he knew flew out of the window.

"N-e-c-c-e-s-a-r-y," said Zanna.

"Wrong!" Jake said, triumphantly. "It's one 'c' and two 's's."

Jake was determined to do better than Zanna in tomorrow's test and he spent the rest of the evening learning spellings.

"You're taking this test very seriously," said Mum at bedtime.

"I want to do well," Jake replied.

"Are you sure you don't just want to beat your sister?" Mum asked.

Jake quickly shoved his toothbrush in his mouth so that he wouldn't have to answer. His mother went on. "You know that co-operation is better than competition?"

Jake pretended not to hear and scrubbed his teeth until white foam spewed out of his mouth. Mum didn't know what it was like to be a twin. People always expected you to be the same in everything and when you weren't they commented and compared. He was better than Zanna at maths but in every subject Zanna beat him in tests.

On the way to school next morning Jake's mouth was dry and he could feel a familiar twitching in his stomach. 'Butterflies' some people called it, but it felt more like pigeons flapping in his stomach. Zanna was going on about their cousin's wedding next week and should she wear her pink strappy sandals or her flip flops. As if he cared!

Suddenly there was a screech of brakes behind them and a piercing yelp. They spun round to see a dog lying whimpering by the side of the road and a car pulling away at great speed. There was no one else around.

Jake and Zanna ran to the dog and squatted down next to it. One of its back legs was twisted at an unnatural angle.

"Poor thing," sobbed Zanna. "That car hit it and the driver didn't even bother to stop." Jake noticed that his sister's hand was trembling as she reached out to stroke the dog's head. Calmly, he told her, "You stay with the dog and I'll go and tell Mr. Chang."

Zanna grabbed his arm. "But what if the dog begins squealing or yelping again? What if it dies? What shall I do?"

"Just talk to it in a quiet voice," he said, reassuringly. "I won't be long."

Jake walked back a block to Mr. Chang's shop. The shopkeeper was coming out carrying a box of mangoes.

Jake ran up to him. "Mr. Chang!" he said. "There's a dog in the road ... back there." He turned and pointed. "A car hit it and it's hurt and we don't know what to do."

Mr. Chang put down the box. "Wait here," he said and he disappeared into the back of the shop. A few moments later he reappeared with his wife.

"Mrs. Chang knows what to do with sick animals," he explained. "She will go with you."

Mrs. Chang crouched down beside the dog and gently felt it all over. She looked carefully at its eyes and inside its mouth before she looked up and smiled at the two children.

"He's going to be OK," she assured them. "His leg is broken but everything else seems all right."

Then she stood up. "I'll get Mr. Chang to help me take him back to the shop where I can put a splint on the leg. And I'll put up a notice asking the owner to come and collect him."

She looked over at the two school bags that Jake and Zanna had dropped when they first ran to the dog. "You did well to get help for the dog," said Mrs. Chang. "Now you had better get on to school."

Jake nodded and asked, "But can we come into the shop on the way home to see how the dog is?"

"Of course you can," said Mrs. Chang, cheerfully. "It will be a treat to see two such kind children."

The twins set off quickly down the road. They were going to be late and Jake wondered whether Mr. Richards would believe their story about the injured dog.

# Part 2

Jake and Zanna walked nervously into the classroom. To their surprise, Mr. Richards beamed at them. "Hello you two. Come in and sit down."

Why was he being so jolly? Latecomers were usually met with sharp words about the importance of punctuality.

Then Mr. Richards addressed the whole class. "Jake and Zanna have a good reason for being late. On the way to school they saw a dog which was hit by a car, and they behaved very responsibly. They asked Mr. Chang, a shopkeeper, for help and, as he didn't want them to get into trouble for being late, he telephoned the school to explain."

Everybody turned to look at the twins. Jake felt his face go hot.
"And now," said Mr Richards, "it's time for the spelling test."
Jake's heart pounded. The spelling test! He'd forgotten all about it.
Mr. Richards continued. "Today, for a change, I want you to work in pairs, helping each other to remember or to work out the correct spellings."

Zanna smiled at Jake. "Be my partner?" she asked.

Jake nodded.

Each time Mr. Richards read out a word, one of the twins would write it out.

Zanna wrote b-a-t-t-e-r-r-y.

"I think battery has one 'r'," said Jake.

Zanna crossed out an 'r'.

Jake wrote t-h-r-o-u-h.

"You've missed out the 'g'," said Zanna.

Jake noticed that his heart wasn't pounding and all the things he knew had stayed inside his head.

When Mr. Richards wrote up the correct spellings and the tests were marked by different children, Zanna and Jake were the only pair in the class to have got every one right.

Jake grinned at his sister. "Because I was working with you I wasn't in a panic," he whispered.

"We're a good team," she replied. "I got in a panic over the dog but you kept calm and made everything all right."

Jake realised that she was right. Then he remembered what Mum had said. "Co-operation is better than competition," he declared – and Zanna gave him a thumbs up sign.

## Comprehension Questions

1 Find 5 adverbs in the text.

2 What does Jake mean when he says "'Butterflies' some people call it ..."?

3 How does Zanna react when they are with the injured dog? How do you know? How does Jake react? How are they different?

4 Why is Mrs. Chang going to put up a notice?

5 What lesson does Jake learn in the story?

6 What do you think will happen when the children go to visit the dog after school? Write the next part of the story.

**Main teaching points**
• Spelling   • Adverbs

# Magic of the earth

Can you buy or sell the sky?
Can you ever touch its blueness
Or its newness in the morning?

Clouds drifting, can you catch them?
Match them? Choose the one you want
To hang above your garden giving shade?

Sunlight streaming down a hillside
Can you put it in a jar
Take it far and pour it over your own back yard?

Can you take the silence of the night
To calm your room in the middle of a busy day?

Can you take a colour from the rainbow
And wrap its softness about your
   shoulders?

Can you take the freshness of the
   mountain air
To bring alive your city street?

Can you know the magic of the earth
And let it be ...

For another day and all the world to
   share?                          **Leonie Bennett**

## Comprehension Questions

1  Find 5 abstract nouns in the poem.

2  How is the last verse different from all the others?

3  Which of the things in the poem would you like to do and why?

4  Which phrase do you think the poet would like you to remember? Why?

5  What is the lesson the poet wants us to learn?

6  Write another 3-line verse of your own.

**Main teaching points**
• Abstract nouns

50

# Creatures of the night

Did you know that, when you are asleep, there is a great deal of activity in the animal world? Animals are hunting and mating and keeping in touch with each other. All this is happening just outside your bedroom window as well as in the countryside, the desert and the rainforest. If you listen carefully you might hear hoots and honks and hiccups and howls. You might even hear an animal laughing …

## Do hyenas really laugh?

Hyenas go hunting in their packs at night and they make a wide variety of strange sounds to keep in touch with each other. The sounds include whoops and cackles and grunts and moans, but when you add it all together it sounds as if they are giggling and guffawing.

Hyenas live in the Sahara Desert in Africa. They usually hunt in a group called a clan which can include up to 70 adults. They normally eat zebras, wildebeest and buffalo. The Hyenas' closest relative is the mongoose and the cat.

## Do wolves really howl at the moon?

Wolves howl, but not at the moon. They join in howling when they hear other wolves at night. They often howl for several minutes, but they do it whether or not the moon is shining. It is possible that their howling may be the signal for them to start hunting.

Wolves are closely related to dogs and are very intelligent creatures.

## Do howler monkeys howl?

Yes they do. Howler monkeys live in South America and they howl in a chorus, like wolves. They do this just before it gets dark to let all the other monkeys know where their territory is. The howling is so loud that it can be heard five kilometres away.

## Why do frogs and crickets make noises at night?

Crickets make a chirping noise at night as a way of attracting a mate. Tree frogs do the same, but they make a huge variety of noises. They peep and whistle and honk and click and sing.

## Are bats blind?

Bats are not blind, but they cannot see very well and they use their ears to tell them where things are. When they are hunting in the dark, they make little noises. Then they judge where an insect or an object is by working out how long it takes for the sound to hit it and for the echo to come back to them. This is called 'echolocation'.

## Why do slimy creatures like the night?

Some creatures, such as slugs and snails, have slimy bodies which help them to move easily along the ground. Frogs have slimy bodies which help to stop them drying out. All these creatures risk drying out in the hot sun, so they prefer night-time when the air is cool and damp.

# How are owls able to hunt at night?

There are several reasons why owls can catch their prey at night. Firstly, they have very good eyesight, and although they cannot move their eyes in their eye sockets at all, they can turn their heads in almost any direction. They can almost turn their heads upside down!

Owls also have excellent hearing. Their ear holes are very big and they can pick up the tiniest of sounds. Some owls catch their prey in complete darkness using sound alone.

Lastly, they can fly silently. There are fine fringes on the edge of their wings that soften any wind noise as they swoop on their prey.

Did you know that owls swallow their prey whole? They then cough up a pellet containing the parts they cannot eat, such as the bones and fur.

## Comprehension Questions

1 Make a list of all the onomatopoeic words in the text which represent animal sounds.

2 Find synonyms in the text for these words: laughing, creatures, group, clever.

3 Look at the word 'echolocation'; how could you work out what it means?

4 Make a glossary to explain what these words mean: swoop, prey, echolocation.

5 Write 5 quiz questions to which the answers can be found in this text. Use them to make up a class quiz.

6 What noises do you hear at night?

**Main teaching points**
• Similes  • Onomatopoeia

# The jaguar and the deer

*This is one of the stories told by the descendants of the Mayan people in Belize. It is said that the story is really about the Spanish invaders and the Mayas. 'Jaguar' stands for the Spanish invaders and 'Deer' stands for the Mayas.*

It happened that a deer and a jaguar both decided to build themselves a house at the same time and in the same place in the rainforest.

Jaguar was looking around when he came across a clearing. 'This looks like a good spot to build a house,' he thought, and he moved a few stones and sticks, then went away to hunt for his next meal.

Along came the deer. 'This looks like a good place to make a home,' he thought. 'There is already a clear space.' Then he worked for a long time, clearing the ground with his antlers.

Next morning, Jaguar returned with some long sticks. He saw that the ground had been cleared and said to himself, 'Someone has been helping me. How kind.' Then he set up a framework for the house which included two rooms – one for him and one for whoever was helping him.

While Jaguar was out hunting that night, Deer came back to the clearing and was astonished to see the shape of a house. 'I have a friend,' he thought. 'Someone who wants to help me and who wants to share my home with me.' Feeling pleased, he covered the house with branches and dry grass so that it would be warm and dry. Then he went into one of the rooms and fell asleep.

When Jaguar returned from hunting, he was delighted to see that the house was finished and he went into the other room, where he too lay down and fell asleep.

Later that day the two housemates awoke and happened to come out of their rooms at the same time. Cautiously, they nodded to each other.

"Thank you for your help," said Jaguar.

"And thank you for your kind assistance also," said Deer, nervously.

"As we have co-operated in building this excellent house together," said Jaguar, "so let us share it. I will go out hunting and you can clean the house and fetch water for when I return."

Deer agreed and happily cleaned the house and fetched water while Jaguar was away. Imagine his horror when Jaguar came back dragging a deer that he had killed.

"Come, my friend," invited Jaguar. "Come and share my meal."

Deer shook his head. "N-n-not hungry ... th-th-thank you," he stuttered.

Poor Deer didn't sleep a wink that night. As soon as dawn broke he went out and searched the forest until he found another jaguar, sleeping on a low branch. Then he went looking for a very large bull whom he knew lived deep in the forest.

"I just met a jaguar who was bad-mouthing you," he told the bull.

"Nobody bad-mouths me and gets away with it!" roared Bull. "Where is the miserable fool?"

"Back there," said Deer, indicating with his antlers, "resting on a low branch."

Fierce with fury, Bull pounded off. Snorting with rage, he dragged the sleeping jaguar to the ground, gored him to death and then lumbered off into the forest.

Deer dragged the dead creature back to the home he shared with Jaguar. "Come, my friend," Deer called to his housemate. "Come and share my meal."

Jaguar shook his head. "N-n-not hungry ... th-th-thank you," he stuttered.

That night Jaguar lay awake, thinking about the deer killing jaguars, while in the next room Deer lay, shaking at the thought of the jaguar killing deer. When, in the early hours, a twig snapped outside the house, Jaguar and Deer each leaped out of their rooms in terror. One fled to the right and the other raced to the left, and so the deer and the jaguar went their separate ways and never shared a home again.

One way to interpret this story: *The Mayas (Deer) had homes in Belize and when the Spanish invaders (Jaguar) came along the Mayas hoped that they could live together.*

*Soon the Mayas realised that the Spanish lived by exploiting and killing them (just as jaguar exploits and eats deer). The Mayas tried to get help from other stronger tribes (just as Deer gets help from Bull).*

*In this story, Deer is not killed so we are told that the Mayas were not completely wiped out by the Spanish. Indeed they used their wits in order to survive.*

## Comprehension Questions

1 Rewrite the first 2 sentences of the introduction in the active voice.

2 Make up your own definitions of these words: descendants, clearing, co-operate, bad-mouthing, invaders. Then check them in the dictionary or with your teacher.

3 Why did Jaguar and Deer nod to each other 'cautiously'?

4 Why did Deer tell Bull that the other jaguar had been bad-mouthing him?

5 What do you understand by the phrase 'used their wits in order to survive'?

6 Summarise the story. Retell it to a partner in no more than 5 sentences.

**Main teaching points**
• Summary  • Passive tense

# Real-life heroes and heroines

**Eugenia Charles** – prime minister
of Dominica from 1980 to 1995

Eugenia Charles was born in 1919 in Pointe Michel, Dominica, the
granddaughter of slaves. She grew up to be the first woman lawyer on
Dominica and the first woman prime minister in the Caribbean.

She thinks that it is important to listen to other people and not just to
tell them what to do – even if you are prime minister. This is something
Eugenia learned as a child, and here is what she says about the way she
was brought up:

> "We were allowed, as children, to give our views. You know, one of the
> things that I think helped [me to get where I did] ... we always sat
> together for meals, parents and children. And ... there was no silence at
> the table; everyone giving their point of view. You didn't always agree
> with ... your father ... but you were not prevented from stating what
> your opinions were.
>
> And you listened to other people's opinions. And the other thoughts
> brushed off on yours, and made you pause, sometimes change your
> mind, and take a different point of view. And I think that was important
> – nobody thinking that you were too stupid, or a child – you had the
> right to talk. You were given as much freedom to talk and to express
> your point of view as if you were a grown-up."

## Clive Lloyd – captain of the West Indies cricket team from the mid-70s until 1985

Clive Lloyd is one of the most respected figures in world cricket. He was born on 31st August 1944 in Georgetown, Guyana and played his first test match in India when he was 22 years old. While he was captain of the West Indies side it was the best team in the world. Clive played in 110 test matches and 87 one-day internationals and lifted the World Cup in 1975 and 1979.

When he was a young boy Clive was encouraged to play by his cousin, West Indies player, Lance Gibbs. He also admired Garfield Sobers. When he was asked what his best moment in cricket was, he answered: "There are many: your first test is always an aim as a youngster – your first test century and the first win as captain. Another was winning the first World Cup and scoring a hundred in the final – that was another first."

## Bob Marley – Jamaican reggae singer, songwriter and musician

Bob Marley was a kind, peace-loving reggae singer whose group, Bob Marley and the Wailers, was the only Jamaican group to have become worldwide superstars.

Bob was born on 6th February 1945 in St. Anns, Jamaica, where he lived until he was 10. Then he moved to Trenchtown, Kingston which was a tough area. It was there that he started to see that the world was unjust. From then on he challenged what he thought was wrong and spoke up for what he thought was right. He sang about poor people in Jamaica and their Rastafarian religion. Bob wanted people to live together in peace and he said in an interview that, "Ras Tafari is the leader … No man can lead man … we have to have unity."

In April 1978, he played the One Love Peace Concert in Kingston, and brought together the two leaders of the Jamaican political parties. At this time there was violent fighting between the supporters of the two parties, and Bob hoped that his concert might help to bring peace between them. For this brave attempt, Bob was given a United Nations Peace award.

In 1980, *Bob Marley and the Wailers* played a concert at Zimbabwe's Independence celebrations to an audience of 40,000. The next year Bob died of cancer at the age of 36. He was buried with his guitar and his bible.

Bob Marley's name made Jamaican music famous all over the world. He was a fantastic performer, a great singer and superb songwriter – as well as a good human being.

## Comprehension Questions

1   Why is each of these people heroic? Using 2 sentences per person summarise the information in this text.

2   **a** Why does Eugenia Charles think it is important to sit together at meals?

   **b** Do you agree with her? Why?

3   In the text about Eugenia Charles find 2 examples of each of these:

   **a** present tense verbs

   **b** verbs in the simple past tense

   **c** verbs in the passive voice

   **d** verbs in the active voice

4   If you were a great cricketer, which of Clive Lloyd's 'best moments' would you most like to achieve? Why?

5   What do you think Bob Marley meant when he said, "No man can lead man ... we have to have unity."

6   'Bob Marley was buried with his guitar and his bible.' What does this tell you about him?

**Main teaching points**
• Verb tenses   • Active and passive voice   • Summary

Answers to puzzles on page 17

6 # HABRX RIPTHDAX

7